IGNITE

The Power in You

Life Book

For: _____

Dated: _____

This is Your story...autograph it with
excellence!

B reak through to your Brillance

E xcellence becomes a Habit

L ead with your Vision

I nvest in Yourself

E mpowering Greatness

V ictory is Inevitable

E nthusiasm for Life

R esponsible for my Actions

S acrifice to make it Happen

H appMEness begins inside ME

I gnite your heart's Desire.

P ersevere with Passion.

IGNITE

The Power in You

If there was ever a time
to Dare, to Believe in You,
to reach out and make
a difference, the time is
now. . .Today.

Empower your Confidence
that lies deep inside.
Follow that Inspired thought
that tugs at your heart,
and let your FAITH
Lead the way.

Ignite the Power in You.

Embrace your Vision
and the Impact your
Dreams will make.
Believe there is no limit
to what You Can Do.

Melanie A. Brown

I
Aspire to BE...

_____

_____

_____

_____

What if You
Realized How
Powerful You
Truly Are...

_____

_____

_____

_____

_____

My Expertise...

_____

_____

_____

_____

_____

_____

_____

I AM...

Ignites the Power in You.

Break through to
YOUR BRILLIANCE

Y Why
am I Here?

C Courage
to get out of the cage

A Attitude
of Gratitude

G Greatness
to begin

E Enthusiasm
to never give up

LEGACY
Begins....

BRILLIANT
Simplicity is the key to Brilliance.

My Affirmation...

When the voice
and the vision on the inside
become more profound,
loud and clear,
than the opinions on the outside,
you have mastered
your Life.

Dr. John Demartini

My Legacy Begins with
WON IDEA...
GRATITUDE

I am so Happy and Grateful for...

Gratitude turns what I have
into enough and more,
it creates a powerful Breakthrough.
Leadership begins with
Gratitude

...when you are Grateful, fear disappears and abundance appears.

GRATEFUL

Success comes from taking initiative and following up...persisting...eloquently expressing the depth of love. What simple **ACTION** could you take today to produce powerful momentum in **your life.**

My Simple Action...I CAN DO THIS...

_____

_____

_____

_____

_____

_____

We tend to find ourselves taking the known way rather than the unknown, only because it is more comforting and less challenging. To give anything less than your Best, is to sacrifice your Gift.

ACT...

Vision without Action is a daydream. Action is the secret to Success; no matter what you do Begin It...

Surround Yourself With
GREATNESS

Name:
Expertise:

Name:
Expertise:

Collaboration is a powerful Success tool.

Name:
Expertise:

Name:
Expertise:

That instills Confidence in the Dream Team.

Name:
Expertise:

Name:
Expertise:

Surround yourself with the
Dreamers and the Doers,
the Believers and the Thinkers;
but most of all,
surround yourself with those who
see Greatness within you,
even when you don't see it in
yourself.

Edmund Lee

CONFIDENT

Every time we face our fear, we gain strength, courage and Confidence.

IMAGINATE...

The World is but a canvas to the Imagination.

REACH UP 10%...

What would you do if the
World would Collaborate to help
you get it done...
To create, one must first be
inspired to Dream of the possibilities,
to Imagine the details
and Believe in the
finished Vision.

Are you creating the Life
You want to Lead?

everything changes...

When you make a change,

Write 2 Aspirations that will
Ignite a Powerful Belief in
Your Potential.

What are your 5 Business Goals
within the next 3 months...

VISIONARY

Be the Change you want to see in the world. Mahatma Gandhi

Perceived failure is oftentimes **Success** trying to be Born in a
Bigger Way.

I need to Persevere in this Area of my Life, and take ACTION...

start your

NEW

LIFE

Most people have achieved their Greatest Success, just one step Beyond their greatest failure...Persevere

Napoleon Hill

Care more than others think wise.
Risk more than others think safe.
Dream more than others think practical.
Expect more than others think possible.

Expand your circle of Compassion and Influence.

Fear grows out of the things we think,
the thoughts we carry in our mind.
Compassion grows from who we are,
and lives in our **hearts**.

CARING....
Care more than others think wise.

We achieve inner Health
only through **Forgiveness...**
The forgiveness not only for others,
but also for ourselves.

forgive to live...

I need to forgive myself for:

_____

_____

_____

_____

_____

_____

The weak can never forgive. Forgiveness is the attribute of the strong.

I need to forgive a loved one for:

_____

_____

_____

_____

_____

_____

FORGIVE...

Forgiveness is a gift you give yourself. Tony Robbins

When things go wrong,
great leaders take full

Responsibility

for the results...No Excuses

MESPONSIBLE...**I need to take more
Responsibility in these areas of my Life...**

i believe
That our background and
circumstances may have influenced
who we are, but we are responsible
for who we become.

RESPONSIBLE

You are only responsible for your life choices and decisions.

People will forget what you said,
they will forget what you did,
but people never forget
how you made them feel.

Maya Angelou

HappMEness,
it starts within ME and shines out to You.

I will lighten up in this part of my life...

_____
_____
_____
_____
_____
_____

Let your SMILE
change the world
But don't let
the world
change your
Smile.

LAUGH

What soap is to the body, laughter is to the Soul.

A positive attitude
causes a chain reaction of
positive thoughts,
events and outcomes.
It is a catalyst and it sparks
extraordinary results.

Wade Boggs

How would I describe my Attitude?

What can I do to make it better?

Leadership is influencing and
Empowering.

EMPOWERED

To Empower another is to Empower yourself.

My
Top Priorities ARE. . .
invest in yourself

Emphasize

family
faith
friends

you

Energize

body
mind
spirit

health

For everything you have missed you have gained **something else,** And for everything you have gained, you lose something else. It is about your priorities in life...You can either regret or **Rejoice.**

IGNITE

the power in you

Prioritize

personal
business
social

life

ENTHUSIASM is one of the most powerful engines of success. When you do a thing, do it with all your might. Put your whole soul into it. Stamp it with your own personality. Be active, be energetic, be **enthusiastic** and **faithful**, and you will accomplish your object. Nothing great was ever achieved without enthusiasm.

Ralph Waldo Emerson

How would I describe my Personality?

How would I rate my Leadership Ability?

How would I rate my Enthusiasm?

I need to Celebrate this in my Life...

Enthusiasm is the Greatness
that Powers Your Soul and the Faith to Believe You Can.

Melanie A. Brown

ENTHUSIASTIC...

Nothing great was ever Achieved without Enthusiasm.

Let your **Dreams** be bigger than
your Fears and your Actions be
bigger than your Words.

What would you do if the world would collaborate to help you get it done?

_____

_____

_____

_____

_____

Miracles start to
happen when you give as much
energy to your dreams
as you do to your fears.

Richard Wilkins

How would this Accomplishment impact your Life?

_____

_____

_____

_____

_____

You are never given a Dream without also being given the Power to make it come true.
Richard Bach

Live in such a way that if anybody would speak bad of you, no one would Believe it.

phenomenal leadership attributes:

HONESTY Respect
INTEGRITY
Loyalty **Courage**
Confidence

How well do I communicate with others?

How well do I listen?

There is a powerful driving force inside every human being that, once unleashed, can make any vision, dream or desire a reality.

You were given this phenomenal Life because you are powerful enough to Live It.

PHENOMENAL

What if everybody participated to create a **vision and purpose** and worked to create it over a period of time to where they really owned it—they felt it—this is our vision—we share it **together.**

Steven R. Covey

It's time to take the LEAD in this part of my Life...

A Leader is one who sees more than others see, who see's farther than others see, and who see's before others do.

Leroy Eims

There is no Leadership Success without
Dedication and Action...

If you don't go after what you want, you'll never have it.
If you don't ask, the answer is always No.
If you don't step forward, you'll always be in the same place.

Nora Roberts

STATE OF MIND

DRIVEN

I will become more dedicated in this area of **my life**...

"The Speed of Success"

I will ask...

I will step forward...

**There are 86,400 seconds in a day.
It's up to you to decide what to do with them.
Dedication makes it happen.**

DEDICATED....

The fuel that powers Your Soul to Never giving up. Melanie A. Brown

I Believe...

_____

_____

_____

_____

_____

_____

_____

_____

_____

_____

Believe in yourself
and all that you are.
Know that there is
something inside you
that is greater
than any obstacle.

Christian D. Larson

YOU were born with wings
YOU were born with ideals and dreams
YOU were born with Greatness
YOU are not meant for crawling so don't...

You have wings...
learn to use them and *fly*

Rumi

I WILL...
Ignite the Power in Me.

Dream

Canvas

Ignite the Power in You...

_____

_____

_____

_____

_____

_____

_____

_____

_____

_____

_____

Believe In Yourself.

This is the beginning of a new day.

God has given me this day to use as I will.

I can waste it or use it for good.

What I do today is important,
because I am exchanging a day of my life for it.

When tomorrow comes, this day will be gone forever,
leaving in its place something that I have traded for it.

I want it to be gain, not loss; good, not evil;
success, not failure; in order that I shall
not regret the price I paid for it.

I am so
Happy
and Grateful for...

_____

_____

_____

_____

_____

_____

_____

_____

_____

_____

_____

_____

You can't start the next chapter of your life
If you keep rereading the last one.

Decide
that you want it
more than
you are
Afraid of it.

Bill Cosby

IGNITE
The Power in You

Take a step
Outside of your
Comfort zone.

Reach Out…

Keep taking Action
and keep learning
from your
mistakes.
Everything will be
within your reach.

IGNITE
The Power in You

I am so
Happy
and Grateful for...

_____

_____

_____

_____

_____

_____

_____

_____

_____

_____

_____

Do It Now...

*Don't wait until
everything is
just right.*

It will never be perfect.

*There will always be
challenges,obstacles and
less than perfect conditions.*

So What.

Get started now.

*With each step you take,
you will grow stronger
and stronger, more and
more skilled, more and
more self-confident
and more and more
successful.*

Mark Victor Hansen

Today
Is the Day...

_____

_____

_____

_____

_____

_____

_____

_____

_____

_____

_____

_____

_____

_____

Did I Make a Difference?

Your gifts are not about YOU
Leadership is not about YOU
Your purpose is not about YOU
A life of significance is about
SERVING
those who need your gifts,
your leadership,
your purpose.

Kevin Hall

IGNITE
The Power in You

Meet with your
Dream Team and
Make it Happen.

Take Massive Action.

Knowing
is not enough,
We must APPLY.
Willing
is not enough,
We must DO.

Bruce Lee

IGNITE
The Power in You

Share your Gifts with others.

Help someone accomplish their Dreams.

Life's most persistent and urgent question is, "What are you doing for others?"

Martin Luther King, Jr.

IGNITE
The Power in You

GO GET IT.

Everything you want
is out there waiting
for you to ask.
Everything you want
also wants you.
But you have to
take action to get it.

Jules Renard

Action creates Satisfaction.

Advice from a Tree

Stand Tall And Proud.
Sink Your Roots
Into the Earth.
Be Content With
Your Natural Beauty.
Go Out on a Limb.
Drink Plenty of Water.
Remember Your
Roots.
Enjoy the View.

I am so
Happy
and Grateful for...

_____

_____

_____

_____

_____

_____

_____

_____

_____

_____

_____

_____

_____

Results show up when You Do.

Let your
light shine.
Be a source of
strength and courage.
Share your wisdom.
Radiate love.

Wilfred Peterson

IGNITE
The Power in You

Be someone's source
of Courage
and Strength.

Share Your Wisdom.

KEEP GOING

YOU *CAN* DO THIS!

IGNITE
The Power in You

We don't pay the price for Success, we pay the price for failure.

If you fail to plan...you plan to fail.

Live Your
Life as an
Exclamation
not an
Explanation.

Jafree Ozwald

IGNITE
The Power in You

I am so
Happy
and Grateful for...

_____

_____

_____

_____

_____

_____

_____

_____

_____

_____

_____

_____

_____

_____

Never underestimate the Power in You.

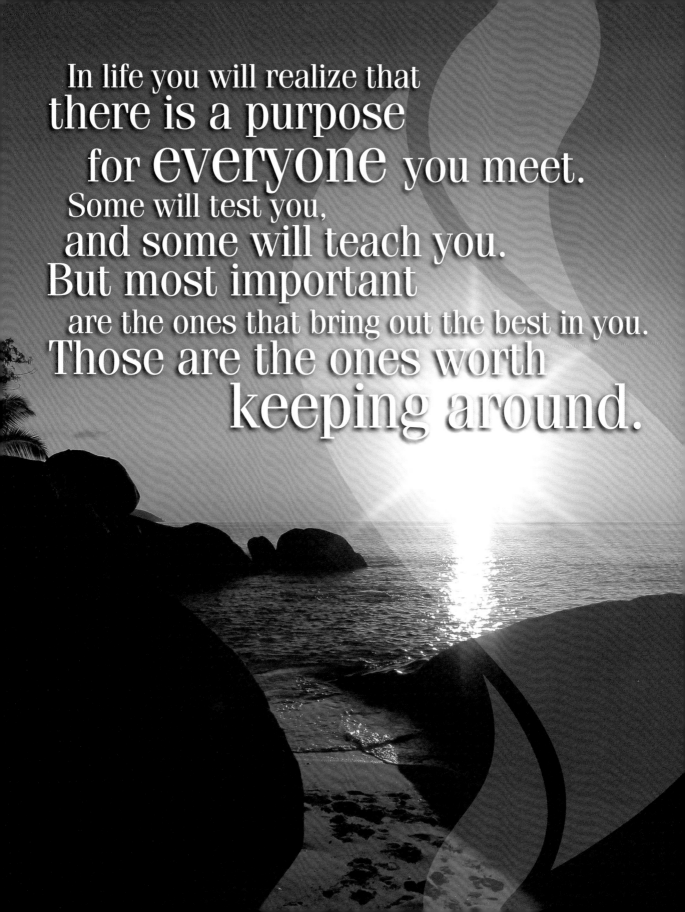

In life you will realize that
there is a purpose
for everyone you meet.
Some will test you,
and some will teach you.
But most important
are the ones that bring out the best in you.
Those are the ones worth
keeping around.

What is your
Purpose for today?

Invest in Your Vision.

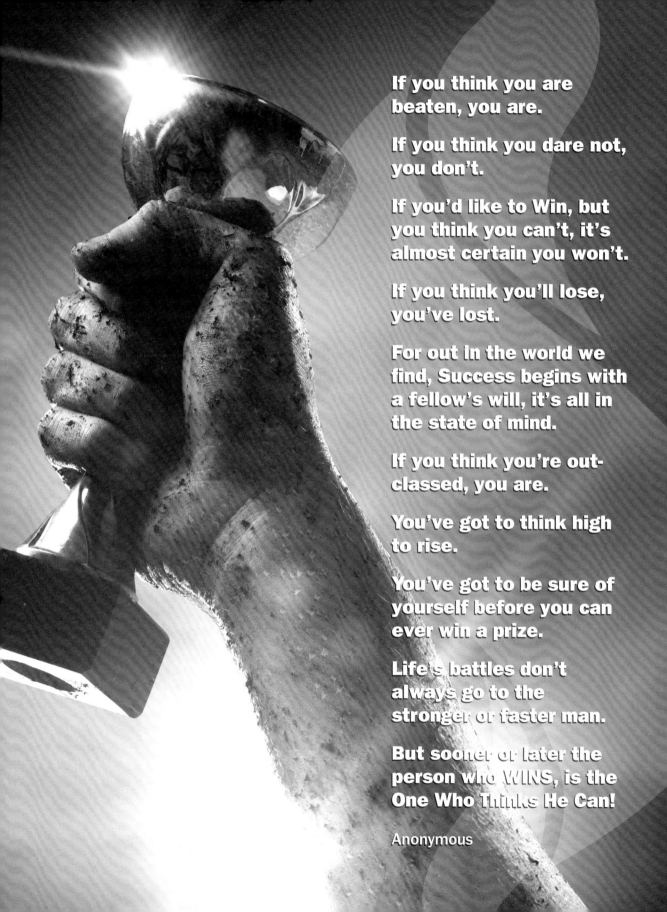

If you think you are beaten, you are.

If you think you dare not, you don't.

If you'd like to Win, but you think you can't, it's almost certain you won't.

If you think you'll lose, you've lost.

For out in the world we find, Success begins with a fellow's will, it's all in the state of mind.

If you think you're out-classed, you are.

You've got to think high to rise.

You've got to be sure of yourself before you can ever win a prize.

Life's battles don't always go to the stronger or faster man.

But sooner or later the person who WINS, is the One Who Thinks He Can!

Anonymous

Listen to your Heart.

_____

_____

_____

_____

_____

_____

_____

_____

_____

_____

_____

_____

_____

_____

Do what it tells you to Do.

One. . .

One tree can start a forest;

One smile can begin a friendship;

One hand can lift a soul;

One word can frame the goal;

One candle can wipe out darkness;

One laugh can conquer gloom;

One hope can raise your spirits;

One touch can show you care;

One life can make the difference—

Be that ONE today.

Mac Anderson

I am so
Happy
and Grateful for...

_____

_____

_____

_____

_____

_____

_____

_____

_____

_____

_____

_____

_____

Be Thankful for all you have!

GRATITUDE Rock

PUT IT IN YOUR POCKET OR PURSE
AND EVERY TIME YOU TOUCH IT,
THINK ABOUT ALL THE THINGS YOU
ARE THANKFUL FOR.

IF YOU ARE HAVING A BAD DAY,
THINK OF ALL THE BLESSINGS IN YOUR LIFE
AND WHAT LIFE WOULD BE LIKE WITHOUT THEM.
YOU WILL BEGIN TO FEEL BETTER RIGHT AWAY.

A GRATITUDE ROCK IS A VERY UNIQUE AND
PERSONAL KEEPSAKE. IT SERVES AS A
REMINDER THAT WE ARE TO BE THANKFUL
FOR ALL THAT WE HAVE.

I Promise Myself...

_____

_____

_____

_____

_____

_____

_____

_____

_____

_____

_____

_____

_____

_____

To be the best that is in ME!

Gratitude
unlocks the fullness of **Life**.
It turns what we have
into enough, and more.
It turns denial into acceptance,
chaos into **order**,
confusion into **clarity**.
It turns problems into **gifts**,
failures into **success**,
the unexpected into perfect timing,
and mistakes into important events.
Gratitude makes sense of
our past, brings **peace** for
today and creates a **vision**
for **tomorrow**.

Melody Beattie

The Power of
Thank You Revolution

I BELIEVE...

...in your worth, in the value it adds to others,
and the value it gives to You, and your
CONFIDENCE TO BELIEVE.

...That tomorrow is a chance to Begin Again,
that failures are the stepping stones to Greatness,
OPPORTUNITIES FOR THOSE WHO BELIEVE.

...That compassion is in the giving of Love and Appreciation,
with an open heart and mind, a feeling of connection to your higher self.
A POWERFUL FORCE TO BELIEVE.

...In your Faith, Family and Friends, the most important people in your life.
They are Angels that lift us to our feet, give us wings to fly, and the
FAITH TO BELIEVE.

...In Your Greatness, to inspire your Dreams and Desires, knowing
ALL THINGS ARE POSSIBLE FOR THOSE WHO BELIEVE.

...that you deserve the Best Life and You Do Make A Difference!
There is something Magnificent about You
that shines through everything You Do...

IT'S TIME TO IGNITE THE POWER IN YOU!

Melanie A. Brown

If you don't have the power to Believe,
take my belief in You, and Make Your Life Shine!

IGNITE
The Power in You

LIFE SCIENCE

Bug
Bites

LIZ HUYCK

TABLE OF CONTENTS

PIONEER VALLEY EDUCATIONAL PRESS, INC

CREEPING, CRAWLING FOOD

Have you heard the joke about the customer who finds a fly in his soup? The customer angrily points it out to the waiter and the waiter says, "Keep your voice down, or everybody will want one!"

OK, so it's an old joke. But is there any truth to it? Who on earth would want to eat a bug?

Would it surprise you that lots of people would? It's true. In many places around the world, eating bugs is no joke. Bugs aren't just pests. They're lunch, dinner, or after-school snacks.

To those of us who have never crunched a cricket or slurped a worm, the idea of eating bugs may sound pretty gross. We wouldn't eat those creepy-crawlies even if someone dared us! But many types of bugs are actually **nutritious**, tasty, and safe to eat.

Eating bugs is an old habit. Long ago, before they learned to farm, our **ancestors** found food by hunting and gathering. This included eating bugs at almost every meal. Back then, bugs were a source of nutrition right under their noses—or buzzing by their ears.

As you've probably noticed, bugs are everywhere. One out of every three animals is a bug. There are about 200 million of the little critters for every person on the planet. No wonder more than half the people on Earth still eat bugs daily.

Of the millions of bugs that we know about, more than 1,900 are somebody's favorite snack. The most popular bugs to eat are crickets and termites, which are said to taste a bit like pineapple, but lots of other bugs are **edible** too.

In Thailand, outdoor markets offer silkworm larvae.

In eastern Africa, grasshoppers are called "flying shrimp."

Restaurants in Mexico sell ant tacos.

Jars of bees line supermarket shelves in Japan.

BUGS DO A BODY GOOD

Think about two plates of food. On one plate is a big, juicy hamburger. On the other is a heaping pile of cooked grasshoppers. Ground beef or bugs— which one do you think is better for your body?

Both have lots of protein, which is what your body uses to build muscle. But in other ways, grasshoppers clearly come out ahead. A pound of grasshoppers has less fat than a pound of beef, and the insects are higher in calcium and iron.

Not only are grasshoppers better for you than beef, they're also better for the planet. It takes a lot of grass, water, and space to raise a cow. How many grasshoppers could be raised on the same amount of land?

And they taste good—a lot like green peppers.

MORE TO EXPLORE

Other bugs are good for you too. A biologist who wrote *The Eat-a-Bug Cookbook* says, "If your bones are still growing,

EAT MORE CRICKETS AND TERMITES."

A MATTER OF TASTE

In North America and Europe, the idea of eating bugs sounds disgusting to most people. But even though we don't think of crickets and termites as food, a lot of what we eat comes from the world of bugs.

Honey is made by bees. Shrimp, crayfish, crabs, and lobsters all belong to a group of animals called **arthropods**, as do bugs.

Other parts of the world have different **taboo** foods. Many people don't eat pork. Lots of people would never eat lobsters or other sea-dwelling "bugs," but they are served at fancy restaurants all over the United States.

How things taste is different even among people who eat insects. People in South Africa might munch termites for lunch, but they'd never eat scorpions, which are raised for food in China. In one part of Southeast Asia, dragonflies are a treat, but in another part, no one would ever think of eating them.

Bugs are considered a perfect food for long space journeys because astronauts can breed them in outer space.

When it comes to eating, people mostly stick with food they're used to. What is seen as food and what is not is a matter of taste—and what you've been taught.

THE BAD BUZZ WITH BUGS

We know that bugs are everywhere. We also know that eating them is good for you and for the planet. And lots of people all over the world think they taste great. So why don't we eat them?

Some people think our feelings about insects come from very long ago. When our ancestors began to raise their own food, insects that feasted on their crops became the bad guys. Over time, we got used to thinking of them as dirty, diseased, and even poisonous.

But most bugs are actually no dirtier than anything else we eat. (Have you ever seen a pig on a farm?) And while it's true that some bugs can spread disease, those aren't the bugs that people eat. Whether it's a bug or a berry, we learn very quickly not to eat foods that can make us sick.

Could our tastes ever change? Could your school lunch ever include grasshopper **kebabs** and caterpillar fritters?

Our feelings about bugs are already changing. If we can get over the gross factor, bugs could one day become part of our daily diet.

Still wondering who on earth would want to eat a bug? Better to ask, who wouldn't?

19

GLOSSARY

ancestors
the people from whom a person is descended

arthropods
animals with a segmented body

edible
able to be eaten

kebabs
pieces of vegetables or meat cooked on a skewer

nutritious
promoting good health and growth

taboo
not acceptable to talk about or do

INDEX